CHRONICLES OF PRAISE: THE REST OF THE STORY 2.0

Cheryl Thompson Williams

authorHOUSE®

AuthorHouse™
1663 Liberty Drive
Bloomington, IN 47403
www.authorhouse.com
Phone: 1 (800) 839-8640

Published by AuthorHouse   11/19/2019

ISBN: 978-1-7283-3644-2 (sc)
ISBN: 978-1-7283-3645-9 (hc)
ISBN: 978-1-7283-3643-5 (e)

This book is dedicated to God, for without Him, there would be no peace, joy, and hope. Therefore, there would be no story or book.

And to my fellow travelers on this journey we call life.

O Lord, thou are my God; I will exalt thee, I will praise thy name, for in perfect faithfulness You have done wonderful things, things planned long ago.

—Isaiah 25:1 (NIV)

Contents

Preface xiii

Acknowledgments xv

Mile Marker 1: Hope
    Psalm 71:14 (NRSV) 1

Mile Marker 2: Faith
    2 Corinthians 5:7 (ESV) 5

Mile Marker 3: Courage
    1 Corinthians 16:13 (NIV) 9

Mile Marker 4: The Value of Family and Friends
    John 13:35 (NIV) 13

Mile Marker 5: Communicate Your Thoughts
    Colossians 4:6 (NIV) 17

Mile Marker 6: Read and Believe God's Word
    Psalm 33:4 (NIV) 23

Mile Marker 7: Prayer
    James 5:16 (KJV) 29

Mile Marker 8: The Fruit of the Spirit
    Galatians 5:25 (NIV) 35

Mile Marker 9: Trust God
    Psalm 56:3–4 (NIV) 43

Mile Marker 10: Be Still and Know That I Am God
    Psalm 46:10 (NIV) 47

Mile Marker 11: Acceptance of God's Will
    Romans 8:28 (NIV) 59

Mile Marker 12: The Victory Is Always Won with God
    1 John 5:4 (NAV) 65

Preface

My, how quickly times passes. It has been fifteen years since the publishing of my first book, *Chronicles of Praise: A Life Journey through Death.* It is the story of receiving the news of the terminal diagnosis of cancer for my first husband, Elliott Thompson, and his subsequent death a year later after receiving the diagnosis. I was inspired by the Holy Spirit to write the book to share the twelve mile markers that I was given to get me through the most horrendous event of my life.

My purpose for writing the book was to encourage others who were faced with the devastation of losing a loved one or facing any of life's hard struggles. I have been so blessed by those who read the book and acknowledged how it inspired and encouraged them.

Again, I am being prompted by the Holy Spirit to share how the same mile markers, which were so prevalent then, continue to be even more prevalent in my life now. It is my prayer that my reflections will be a source of encouragement for the difficult times we all must encounter on this life journey.

It is my greatest desire to help you to understand that whatever you may be facing, with God on your side, you have the victory. The fight is fixed, and you will win. I know of what I speak!

Come and travel with me a while as I share what God has taught me and wants me to share with you. The words of Bishop TD Jakes still ring true. "The touch of a fellow traveler lets us know that we are not alone in our struggle."

At the conclusion of each mile marker, I have included some questions called "Journey Reflections," which will encourage you to reflect on your life journey.

Please take the time to answer each question with sincere effort. Remember you only get out what you put in. Your answers may give you some important insight, which may be beneficial as your journey continues.

Acknowledgments

He fills my life with good things.
—Psalm 103:5 (TLB)

What a blessing to be placed in a loving family. It is through your unconditional love that I have traveled so well on this journey called life.

Thomas, your love and support continue to be immeasurable. I thank God for divinely appointing our journeys to meet.

I am eternally grateful for all those God has placed on my journey. You have poured such good into my life. Whether you have traveled with me a long time or you are a newly acquired friend, you are a blessing in my life. I acknowledge you all for the gifts of love, support, encouragement, and especially prayer.

Wanda Dorsey and Phyllis Smith, I am indebted to you for the many times I needed you the most and you were always there.

I am so grateful for God planting me at Zion Hill Baptist Church in Atlanta, Georgia. Pastor Aaron Parker, First Lady Sheila Parker, and my entire Zion Hill family have provided me with a firm spiritual foundation, which has made me a much better person. "Living to love and loving to serve" is much more than a motto. It is my way of life.

Elliott Thompson, my first husband, and Agnes Williams, Thomas's first wife, you have helped to make us the people we are today. Thank you for teaching us how to love and be loved.

Philippians 1:3 (NIV) states it best. "I thank my God every time I remember you."

MILE MARKER 1

Hope

But I hope continually, and will praise you yet more and more.

—Psalm 71:14 (NRSV)

It is no coincidence that hope was the first mile marker in my first book, *Chronicles of Praise: A Life Journey through Death*, for hope is the foundation of life. As long as you have hope, you have life. As long as you have life, you have hope.

In the most difficult of times, you must never give up hope. Without a sense of hope, all will be lost. How can you maintain a sense of hope when you are faced with the hope stealers of life? You must come to know the true source of hope: our Heavenly Father, Jesus Christ, and the Holy Spirit. Having a relationship with the Trinity solidifies your foundation of hope. As the old hymn states, "My hope is built on nothing less than Jesus's blood and righteousness. I dare not trust the sweetest frame but wholly lean on Jesus's name."

Reading and believing God's Word will also build your sense of hope. Seek out the many scriptures that will give you hope. I would like to suggest a few scriptures that have given me hope in the most difficult of times.

But now, O Lord, what do I look for? My hope is in you. (Psalm 39:7 NIV)

Through Him you believe in God, who raised Him from the dead and glorified Him and so your faith and hope are in God. (1 Peter 1:21 NIV)

We remember before our God and Father your work produced by faith, your labor promoted by love, and your endurance inspired by hope in our Lord Jesus Christ. (1 Thessalonians 1:3 NIV)

But those who hope in the Lord shall renew their strength; they shall soar on wings like eagles, they will run and not grow weary, they will walk and not faint. (Isaiah 40:31 NIV)

Be joyful in hope, patient in affliction, faithful in prayer. (Romans 12:12 NIV)

There are so many more that will inspire you to hold on to your hope. Search for them when you need hope the most. No matter what you may be facing, hold on to your hope. For every earthly situation, there is a heavenly solution of hope. Even when you face the death of a loved one, hold tight to the hope of God's love, peace, and comfort. Hold on also to the hope of a joyous reunion with the ones you love so dearly.

Point to Ponder

As long as you have hope, you have life. As long as you have life, you have hope.

Help for

Our

Periods of transition,

Ever grateful for what God will do

Journey Reflections

Consider the following questions for your journey reflection:

Hope

1. What inspires your hope?

2. Find and write down three scriptures from the Bible that speak of hope.

3. Do you have hope for the future? Why or why not?

4. Who or what is your greatest source of hope? Why?

MILE MARKER 2

Faith

For we walk by faith not by sight.
—2 Corinthians 5:7 (ESV)

One of my favorite scriptures is Hebrews 11:1 (NAS). "Now faith is the assurance of things hoped for, the conviction of things not seen." There is an adage that "seeing is believing," but with faith, the opposite is true. Believing produces the seeing.

In order to have faith, you must have hope. When you have hope, then you will have an increase in your faith. Therefore, hope and faith are like twins. While they are not identical, they are strongly bonded for they come from the same source.

Mile marker 1, hope, and mile marker 2, faith, just as when I was dealing with the tragedy of Elliott's death, continue to be essentials for the rest of the story. They have brought me through so many difficult situations.

My faith in God gives me the reassurance of victory. No matter what I must face, I will be victorious. The same is true for you. Faith is like a muscle. If you don't exercise, your muscles will become weak and begin to atrophy. The same is true of your faith. In order for your faith to be strong, it must be exercised. It is easy to claim to have faith when things are going well. But when the stakes are high and your back is against the wall, you know that only God can work things out, and that is the true testing of your faith.

Let me encourage you to put your faith in God, no matter what it looks like or feels like. He is faithful.

When you are in doubt or are afraid, look back over your faith history with the Lord. Faith history is when you know that God has been faithful to you. If you are trying to identify a moment in your faith history, then think about those times when you knew that only God could resolve the issue—and He did.

Perhaps you haven't developed a faith history. Now is the time to begin. It is no coincidence that you are reading these words. God is reaching out to you and wants you to recognize that He is a faithful God. The song "Great Is Thy Faithfulness" still resounds in my soul. I pray that you will come to understand how faithful God is.

Hebrews 11:6 reminds us that without faith, it is impossible to please God. Anyone who comes to Him must believe that He exists, and He rewards those who earnestly seek Him.

Do a faith check now. How strong is your faith?

Point to Ponder

The issues may change, but God's faithfulness never changes.

Father

Always

Inspiring

The journey with

Hope, faithfulness, and favor

Journey Reflections

Consider the following questions for your journey reflection:

Faith

1. What is faith to you?

2. Is it possible to have both faith and fear? Explain your answer.

3. How can you increase your faith?

4. Write an example of a time when your faith brought you through a difficult time.

MILE MARKER 3

Courage

> Be on your guard; stand firm in the faith; be courageous;
> be strong.
>
> —1 Corinthians 16:13 (NIV)

Many think that courage is moving forward without fear. But real courage is moving forward *in spite of* fear or worry.

We were not created to fear or worry. Second Timothy 1:7 serves as a reminder that God has not given us the spirit of fear but power, love, and a sound mind. Believing this provides us with the courage to face any of life's obstacles.

How can this kind of courage be built? We build courage by trusting and remembering that God will never leave or forsake us. We can have confidence in Him, which will give us the courage needed. Remember that no weapon formed against us will prosper. This doesn't mean that weapons won't be formed. They will. It is the job of Satan, our greatest enemy, to do all he can to thwart our belief in our Heavenly Father and His ability to provide all we need, which includes courage.

We must believe in our hearts that God is for us. Fervently withstand enticements to give in to fear and discouragement. There is a sustainable source of courage available at all times. God's Word is our source and resource, whenever courage is needed.

I do not know what the future holds, but I do know who holds the future of us all. That gives me the courage I need to continue the rest of the story. It is my prayer that you will continue your journey with the same formidable courage. Have courage, for God is on our side!

Point to Ponder

Take courage. Life can change in the blink of an eye, but God never blinks.

Constantly

Open to the

Uniqueness of God's

Responses,

Always

Grateful for

Everything He does

Journey Reflections

Consider the following questions for your journey reflection:

Courage

1. Do you have strong courage? Explain your answer.

2. How do you demonstrate your courage?

3. What can be done to gain courage?

4. Name three people who demonstrated courage in difficult situations. Explain how they demonstrated courage.

MILE MARKER 4

The Value of Family and Friends

By this everyone will know you are my disciples, if you
love one another.

—John 13:35 (NIV)

As I continue the rest of my story, I have found mile marker 4 to be
even more valuable. Perhaps with age, I have become more sentimental.
I seem to cherish relationships of family and friends even more.

Having lost both family and friends, I find that the value of these
relationships to me has intensified. I am more focused on how
important they really are. It has become essential that I do not take
these relationships lightly.

I believe that God brings people into our lives for a reason, a season, or
a lifetime. It is our responsibility to love them no matter which category
they are in. One thing that has helped me do that is learning to love
people where they are, not where I want them to be. Acceptance carries
a lot of weight in fostering good relationships.

I cannot imagine how I would have survived Elliott's illness and death if it had not been for God's provision of my family and friends. I continue to be grateful for the blessing of having a blended family as the result of my having a second chance at love with Thomas Williams. The Lord answered my prayers that I would be accepted and loved by the Williams family. I am, just as Thomas is, by my family.

It is amazing to see how Elliott's family embraced and loves Thomas. He, in turn, has a genuine affection for them. Many times this mutual affection among blended families does not develop. It makes me even more grateful. It is vital that I express my appreciation and not assume that they know how much I love them.

Take a few moments and reflect on your family and friends. Are there relationships that need to be mended? When was the last time you truly expressed your love, not only in words but also in addition, through loving acts of kindness?

I have learned that the power of forgiveness, compassion, and grace are mandatory in maintaining good relationships with family and friends. It is also easy to take the people you love for granted. You expect them to always be there. Or you assume that they know how much you care about them. But it is wise not to do that. You never know when they or you must bid farewell for the last time. Therefore, seize every opportunity to express love. Let 1 Corinthians 16:14 (NIV) serve as a strong reminder. "Let all you do be done in love."

Point to Ponder

God chooses our family. We choose our friends. Be sure to find the value and the blessings of both.

Faithfully

Assuring

Me with

Inspiration and

Love

Year around

Affectionately

Nurturing my

Development

Family by choice

Rendering

Ideal

Encouragement

Never

Departing from their loving

Support

Journey Reflections

Consider the following questions for your journey reflection:

The Value of Family and Friends

1. What is the value of family and friends in your life?

2. How do you show your family and friends that they are valued?

3. How do you handle difficult relationships?

4. It is said that some people come into our lives for a reason, a season, or a lifetime. Give an example of each from your life.

MILE MARKER 5

Communicate Your Thoughts

Let your conversation be always full of grace, seasoned
with salt, so that you may know how to answer everyone.
—Colossians 4:6 (NIV)

Words have power. Therefore, it is essential that they be chosen wisely. Communicating your thoughts effectively can make the difference in how relationships are fostered or encumbered. I have found over the years that many times it is not only what you say but also the way that you say it that can make a major difference in how thoughts are communicated.

One of my favorite adages is "Say what you mean and mean what you say." When that statement is honored, communication is enriched. Another important factor in good communication is timing. Evaluate if this is the best time to share the communication. Timing is everything.

Words spoken in anger cannot be taken back, no matter how much one may regret having said them. A good analogy is nails being hammered into a fence. You remove the nails, but the holes are still there. When hurtful words are spoken, the scars remain long after the apology.

Communication of your thoughts can be improved by a simple formula that I taught my students, which has served me well as I have continued on my journey.

E + R = O stands for Event plus Response equals Outcome. Many times there are events in our lives which we have little or no control of. They just happen. But how we respond to those events is what can be controlled. Your response will determine the outcome. Again, the importance of choosing words wisely is mandatory.

Proverbs 15:1 (NIV) can serve as a reminder. "A gentle answer turns away wrath, but a harsh word stirs up anger." In James 1:19–20 (NIV), we are cautioned, "My dear brothers and sisters, take note of this: everyone be quick to listen, slow to speak, slow to become angry, because human anger does not produce the righteousness that God desires."

Seek opportunity to communicate lovingly and with kindness to those you care about and even to strangers, for you never know the burdens that others are carrying. A kind word or a smile can make a big difference in the life of a person who is struggling.

Are there those with whom you need to strengthen the bonds of communication? Don't hesitate to do so. Don't take for granted that you will have a chance to express your feeling at a later time. Tomorrow is not promised to any of us. Communicating lovingly and openly with those in our lives eases the worry of leaving things unsaid when our journeys have ended.

God's love has been communicated to us in so many ways, but none as great as the sacrifice of His Son. One of the ways that we honor His sacrifice is by showing our love for Him as well as love for each other. The words of Ephesians 5:2 (NIV) serve as a powerful reminder. "And walk in the way of love, just as Christ loved us and gave Himself up for us as a fragrant offering and sacrifice to God."

Always be mindful to communicate your thoughts in love.

Point to Ponder

Words have power! Always chose them wisely.

Caringly

Offering

Marvelous

Moments of

Understanding,

Never

Indicating

Callous

Attitudes

Toward

Each other

Journey Reflections

Consider the following questions for your journey reflection:

Communicate Your Thoughts

1. Is good communication a part of your life? Why or why not?

2. What can be done to make communication better in your relationships?

3. How can good communication change, prevent, or correct a problem?

4. Describe a time or situation when poor communication created a problem.

Mile Marker 6

Read and Believe God's Word

For the Word of the Lord is right and true, He is faithful in all He does.

—Psalm 33:4 (NIV)

Just as it was fifteen years ago, mile marker 6 is still the firm foundation on which I have built my life. Reading and believing God's Word has provided courage, comfort, strength, hope, and endurance to continue on even in the face of great adversity. Especially during the times of trials, I would seek out scriptures or would go to church, being really opened to hear God's Word and so willing to believe it. I am always so amazed, though I shouldn't be, that the sermon would be just what I needed to hear. God has a marvelous way of providing just what you need, when you need it. Listening to gospel music in the car or at home throughout the day is another way of receiving God's Word. I believe that music can set the atmosphere for peace and tranquility, if it is chosen wisely.

Words of a song can make a big difference in how your Spirit is being feed. That is one of the reasons you need to choose your music wisely.

Going to weekly Bible study is another source for receiving and believing God's Word. There was a time that I didn't attend Bible Study; little did I know what I was missing. I am grateful that I started going, and now it is a vital part of my life.

If you do not attend a Bible study, let me encourage you to do so. It will provide additional substance to help you maneuver on this sometimes difficult journey we call life.

Our church is blessed to have SOLLAS, which stands for School of Love, Learning, and Service. This is the equivalent of Sunday school, only held on Saturday mornings. One might ask, "Why would you sacrifice sleeping in or postponing weekend events?" Once I started going, I found the answer. It is worth it!

The structure for SOLLAS continues to evolve for greater effectiveness, as it increases in value.

This is another opportunity to study God's Word and share with others in the class and learn from them. The lessons are relative to making us better and stronger people who are all called for a purpose of being here on earth at this particular time. Do you know your purpose? God's Word is a wonderful way to figure out what it is or confirm that you are right.

I love daily devotionals. There are many good ones available. They provide another chance to read and believe God's Word in a short and concise way. Part of my day begins and ends with one of my favorite devotionals, "Jesus Calling," by Sarah Young. She provides words of encouragement in the voice of Jesus speaking in just a few paragraphs with several supportive accompanying scriptures. I am so grateful for the daily inspiration. The readings are a great reminder of how much Jesus loves and cares about me as well as all of His children. There is another devotional that has been a blessing of encouragement: "Be Encouraged: A Daily Devotional, Volume 1," by Gregory A. Johnson.

It is a compact book that offers another opportunity to spend quality time with God and His Word. Don't hesitate to look for well-written devotionals. They will be worth the time you spend reading them.

Let me encourage you to allow the Word of God to make your life journey more comfortable, for the trials and tribulations of life are certain. Reading and believing God's Word will provide you with whatever you may need to be an overcomer.

I stand firm on the saying "If God said it, I believe it." You can too. In the words of Donald Lawrence, one of my favorite singers, "Let the Word do the work", and it will.

Point to Ponder

We can read the Word; study the Word; recite the Word; spread the Word; but most importantly, we must live the Word.

Glorious

Opportunity for

Divine

Salvation

Wisdom

Ordered for

Redemptive

Deliverance

Journey Reflections

Consider the following questions for your journey reflection:

Read and Believe God's Word

1. Do you value reading God's Word? Why or why not?

2. Do you participate in a Bible study? Why or why not?

3. Do you read God's Word daily? Why or why not?

4. What other ways are available to seek God's words?

Mile Marker 7

Prayer

The effective fervent prayer of a righteous man availeth much.

—James 5:16 (KJV)

Prayer has been prevalent throughout my journey. It is the cement that holds all of the mile markers in place. Prayer also holds me in place when the storms of life are wreaking havoc in my life. Prayer has brought me through heartaches, disappointments, pain, and utter chaos. It will do the same for you.

Prayer is the key that unlocks the doors of hope and faith. It is the entrance to the throne of grace. God is there waiting to commune with you, no matter how big or small your issue is.

He loves you so much that whatever concerns you concerns Him. He is a way maker, miracle worker, promise keeper, and light in the darkness. Prayer is your connection to all that power. He wants you to use it.

I have witnessed the power of prayer in my life as well as the lives of others. Prayer has always been important to me, but as I continue with the rest of my journey, it has become even more important. Our prayers are not informing God of anything. He is omnipotent and omnipresent.

What prayer does is demonstrate to God our need of Him. Prayer opens up the lines of communication. He listens to us, and we must be willing to listen to Him. Prayer is a two-way conversation.

He will never leave a prayer request unanswered. We must trust Him and accept His way of answering and His perfect timing. Father really does know best!

As I continue on this journey of life, I have become more willing to pray out loud. There was a time I found it difficult. I didn't have a problem praying silently. How do you feel about praying out loud? Is there a spirit of discomfort? If so, let me share with you how I overcame that discomfort. I became mindful of who I was talking to. Prayer is just a conversation with God, just as you would talk with your best friend. You are just allowing others to listen in on your conversation. When I let go of the fear of being judged by what I was saying or how I was saying it, I became more comfortable and confident in praying out loud. God doesn't sit in judgment of our prayers, so we shouldn't be concerned about how anyone else may feel or think about our praying. Remember that prayer is a wonderful opportunity to encourage others and to take their concerns to the Lord. A prayer can be simple and be just as effective as those that are long and eloquent. There are so many times that I am prompted by the Holy Spirit to pray for someone or some situation. Please be attuned to that prompting. Pray when passing an accident, passing strangers on the street, and in situations where it is apparent that God needs to handle it.

We are so blessed to have a powerful prayer ministry at my church. Individuals are welcomed to come to the chapel for prayer after each service. I have personally benefited from those powerful prayers. Our entire church family is also the beneficiary of that ministry. It is not uncommon to see members praying with and for each other inside and outside of the chapel and the sanctuary. What a beautiful sight to see the people of God praying with and for each other!

It is God's will that we pray for each other. James 5:16 confirms that we should do so. "Therefore confess your sins to one another, and pray for one another, so that you may be healed. The prayers of the righteous is powerful and effective."

According to the *NIV Exhaustive Concordance,* the word *prayer* or a various conjugation of the verb appears 375 times, which is further proof of the importance of prayer. We are also reminded in 1 Thessalonians to pray without ceasing.

While we are praying, let's be mindful to thank God for everything before we ask for anything. There is a powerful order to keep in mind as we continue to pray on this journey: keep God first, people second, and things last. Yes, necessarily in that order.

Praying with my husband is such a wonderful gift. It helps us to remain close to God and each other. One of our greatest blessings is to have a room in our home that we have dedicated as our prayer room. What an awesome way to start the day praying together in there. It is also where we participate on a marvelous prayer line, which God orchestrated our participation. Let me encourage you to seek out a prayer line as another form of connecting with a body of like-minded believers to pray with and for.

The prayer room also serves as a place of solace whenever a sense of peace is needed. We both value prayer so much, for prayer is a privilege that God has provided for us all to commune with Him on a personal level.

When we are confronted with decisions to be made or with dealing with any concerns about the issues in our lives, we are quick to turn to prayer.

We are very diligent about praying for family members, friends, and anyone we know or who has requested prayer. We all are in need of prayer, for everyone is dealing with something in this life.

If you are not praying with your mate or significant other, please do so. If you are, please continue. Prayer makes a difference!

Keeping the lines of communication with God open makes for a much more peaceful journey.

Won't you join me in prayer?

Point to Ponder

It is our job to pray. It is God's job to answer. Trust God to do His job. Make sure we are doing ours.

Power

Released

At

Your

Eagerness to

Respond to God's way

Journey Reflections

Consider the following questions for your journey reflection:

Prayer

1. Do you believe that prayer can change things? (Explain why or why not.)

2. Give an example when you experienced a change in a situation that you prayed about.

3. How often do you pray? (Explain why or why not.)

4. Are you comfortable praying out loud? (Explain why or why not.)

MILE MARKER 8

The Fruit of the Spirit

If we live by the Spirit, let us also keep in step with the
Spirit.

—Galatians 5:25 (NIV)

Just as we need fruit to nourish our bodies, we need the Fruit of the
Spirit to nourish our souls.

This mile marker has been such a major contributor to the successes in
my life. When operating in the Fruit of the Spirit, life is much easier
to handle. My attitude toward people and life in general is better.
Handling difficult situations within the confines of the Fruit of the
Spirit ensures much better outcomes. Showing love, joy, peace, long-
suffering, kindness, generosity, faithfulness, gentleness, and self-control
are essentials for this sometimes tedious life journey.

The Fruit of the Spirit is a precious gift that the Lord has provided for
us to enjoy as we continue on this journey we call life. It can make life
so much sweeter.

Love

Many times, confusion and conflict can be resolved by committing to the essence of the Fruit of the Spirit.

According to many scripture references, love conquers all. The spirit of love can make any situation better. Love is not an option; it is a commandment. God makes it very plain in John 15:12 (KJV). "This is my commandment, that you love one another as I have loved you." John 13:35 (ESV) empathically states, "By this all men will know that you are my disciples, if you have love for one another." God tells us in 1 Corinthians 16:14 (NIV), "Do everything in love."

But I believe that the greatest demonstration of God's love is found in John 3:16 (KJV). "For God so loved the world that He gave His only begotten son that whosoever believeth in Him should not perish but have everlasting life." God is love! Therefore, may we always be mindful to honor God's precious gift by showing love throughout our life journey.

Joy

True joy comes from the Spirit of God within. If you rely on people and things to supply you with joy, you will be disappointed. For that type of joy is fleeting. It will come and then go. The joy of the Lord is consistent, no matter the circumstances. The joy I am speaking of is the one referenced in the song "This Joy That I Have." The lyrics to the song state, "The world didn't give it to me, the world can't take it away."

Live life joyfully, even in the face of difficulty. Rely on the joy of the Lord. There is reassurance in God-given joy that can maintain you no matter what you have to face.

Peace

Peace is not the absence of chaos and conflict but having the presence of God in the midst of the chaos and conflict. The Word says that God will provide the peace that is needed. Philippians 4:7 (NIV) remind us, "And the peace of God, which transcend all understanding, will guard your hearts and minds in Christ Jesus." Always seek God's peace.

Long-suffering

Long-suffering is having patience. In our current microwave mentality world and way of life, we want things quick and in a hurry. But long-suffering requires a willingness to wait on God to respond in His time to our needs. Lamentations 3:25 (NIV) says, "The Lord is good to those whose hope is in Him, to the one who seeks Him." Asking for patience in all areas of our lives is vital as we continue on this often fast-paced journey we call life.

Kindness

One of the greatest gifts that you can give to anyone is kindness. You never know what the people you encounter on this life journey are dealing with. Kindness can make a major difference in a person's life. Even though the encounter may be brief, it may be very profound. Kindness can have a domino effect. Your being kind to someone just may inspire that person to be kind to another person. I remember hearing about a campaign called Random Acts of Kindness. There is even a Random Acts of Kindness day, which is celebrated on February 17. Wouldn't it be wonderful if we celebrated Random Acts of Kindness every day? There is a quote by Martin Kornfeld that beautifully summarizes this thought. He said, "If we all do one random act of kindness daily, we just might set the world in the right direction."

Generosity

True generosity comes from the heart. It is important to have a willing heart to be generous toward others. I believe that we are all blessed to be a blessing to others. When we think about how good God has been to us, it should be so easy to be generous with others. The spirit of your generosity is vital.

Second Corinthians 9:7 (NIV) admonishes us to be cheerful givers, not to give reluctantly or under compulsion. God loves a cheerful giver. We need to show generosity not only through our finances but also through our time dedicated to loving and serving others.

Faithfulness

God is so faithful to us and He deserves our faithfulness toward Him. He also expects us to be faithful toward each other. As I was growing up, my mother instilled in me the importance of the saying, "Your word is your bond." I still adhere to those words today. It is essential that we are faithful in what we say and what we do.

Gentleness

We are reminded in Proverbs 15:1 (NIV) that a soft answer turns away wrath but grievous words stir up anger.

Many conflicts could be abated and even averted by remembering that scripture. Treating people and situations with gentleness can make a profound difference. Having a gentle spirit can be very influential. Be conscience of using gentleness as you continue your life journey.

Self-control

It is so important to exercise self-control as you deal with the issues of life. Many times the lack of self-control can create problems and/ or make situations worst. A sense of discipline/self-control can assist in meeting goals, making good decisions, and building self-confidence. God has given us the power of self-control. We must be careful to effectively use that power, love, and self-discipline. We are admonished in 2 Timothy 1:7 (NIV), "For the Spirit God gave us does not make us timid, but gives us power, love and self-disciple." A sound mind is an indicator of a mind that is disciplined/self-controlled.

The world would be a much better place if we would all live by the Fruit of the Spirit.

Point to Ponder

The Fruit of the Spirit makes life sweet.

Favor

Resulting in

Understanding the

Influence of

Truth

Over

Fear

The

Holy One

Empowering

Superb

Peace

In the

Reliance of an

Intimate

Relationship with

The Savior

JOURNEY REFLECTIONS

Consider the following questions for your journey reflection:

The Fruit of the Spirit

1. List the Fruits of the Spirit. (Think about each one as you write.)

2. What value is there in living according to the Fruit of the Spirit?

3. Which one of the Fruit of the Spirit needs more development in your life? (Explain how you will develop it.)

4. Explain how you can go about developing more of the Fruit of the Spirit in your life.

MILE MARKER 9
Trust God

When I am afraid, I put my trust in you. In God, whose
word I praise, in God I trust; I shall not be afraid. What
can mere mortals do to me?

—Psalm 56:3–4 (NIV)

Mile marker 9 is another foundational truth that has served me so well
as I have traveled along this phenomenal journey called life.

Trusting God is the pinnacle for the rest of my story. It is my prayer that
you too put your trust in the One who loves you so much and wants
you to succeed in this life and to receive the life that is to come, the
One and only God.

Psalm 62:8 (NIV) states it so well, "Trust in Him at all times, you
people, pour out your heart to Him, for God is our refuge."

When you truly trust God, you relinquish total control to Him. That
can be difficult to do, for we as human beings strive to be and stay in
control. However, it is only when you learn to let go and let God that
you will you learn to surrender totally to Him. Only then will you
have the answers you need, the strength to endure, and the confidence
needed that only He can provide.

When you affirm your trust in God, it is like building up the security of having money in a savings account. You save money when times are good so that in times of emergency, you are able to financially handle any issue that arises.

When you deposit trust in God, it is compounded with interest daily. The more you trust Him, the more you are empowered to do so. Building trust in the good times prepares you to be able to trust Him during the storms of life. You can dip into your reserve of trust that you have deposited to get you through whatever life throws at you.

Your trust in God reassures you that He is with you. You have no reason to fear, no matter what the circumstances look like. He has promised that He will not leave or forsake you. You can trust the Promise Maker and the Promise Keeper.

Do you trust God implicitly?

Point to Ponder

When you can't trace His hand, trust His heart.

Total

Reliance

Upon the

Savior

To keep His Word

Journey Reflections

Consider the following questions for your journey reflection:

Trust God

1. How has your trust in God gotten you through a difficult situation? (Give details.)

2. How can you develop greater trust in God? (Explain your answer.)

3. Does trusting God guarantee that all your problems will be resolved? (Explain your answer.)

4. Can your trust in others influence your trust in God? (Explain your answer.)

Mile Marker 10

Be Still and Know That I Am God

Be still, and know that I am God; I will be exalted
among the nations, I will be exalted in the earth!
—Psalm 46:10 (NIV)

Some things never change and will always remain the same. One of the best examples of something that will never change is God's love, nature, and Word.

As I reflect over the original mile markers, I see how mile marker 10 has been a constant reminder of my need to be still, trust God, and acknowledge who He is and what He has the power to do.

I have seen my personal growth in handling life situations being mindful of the importance of this particular mile marker. When I reread mile marker 10 in *Chronicles of Praise: A Life Journey through Death,* I was reminded of an incident that occurred a few days before Elliott's death. It deserves to be shared again. It solidifies the essence of the meaning "Be still and know that I am God."

This is an excerpt taken from the Original Mile Marker 10:

Mile Marker 10 was a respite along the journey, for God profoundly ministered to me just a few days before Elliott died. Being so impacted by what happened compelled me to share the incident at Elliott's home-going service. For I knew without a doubt that God was speaking directly to me through the following occurrence.

There was a strong desire to personally share the lesson, but it would have been too difficult to speak without crying. I requested my dear friend Myrtle Boyer to read it for me in the form of a letter written to those who were in attendance.

Allow me to share this touching story with you …

November 18, 2000

Dear Loved Ones,

I really wanted to share this with you myself, but I was afraid that once I got past the "Dear Loved Ones," you would not be able to understand a word through my crying.

I wanted to take this opportunity to thank each of you for being here as well as to thank those who had the desire to be here but couldn't. Your love and support have sustained us over the past year much more than you could know.

Please be encouraged and do not dwell on Elliott not being with us, but focus on the time he was here. God blessed us with him for fifty-four years. It was a special blessing for me being married to him for twenty-eight of those years.

We all prayed for Elliott's healing and restoration of his body. I just wanted to remind you that God did answer our prayers, maybe not as we wanted in the natural realm but as He knows best.

Elliott touched each of our lives in a very special way, just as we touched his. Please let the good memories of him comfort you when you are overcome with sadness. We have come here to celebrate his life, not mourn his passing.

I wanted to briefly share a wonderful experience that happened just days before Elliott's passing. I felt it really was a message from God to help me prepare for Elliott's leaving.

I am sure God would like for me to share this with you to encourage your hearts.

I looked for my checkbook to balance; it wasn't in my purse where it was usually kept. Now the first thing I did after frantically looking all over the house was to pray that God would help me find it or, if it wasn't found, no financial harm would occur as a result of it being lost. I should have stopped with that prayer. Unfortunately, I allowed fear and panic to set in. By the time my imagination had finished, I was in total financial ruin with someone using a false identification to clean out my checking and savings as well as getting credit cards in my name. With panic building, a trip was made to the last place I had written a check in hopes that some Good Samaritan had found it and turned the checkbook in. But it wasn't there. I went to the credit union to stop payment on the last check that was left in the checkbook. In addition, I wanted to close out my account totally. Fortunately, the service center could not do that. Being told I would have to wait until Monday caused even more concern, for on Monday we were to leave for a trip to a hospital in Mexico and be gone for three weeks. Returning home in a state of total despair, I realized that I just couldn't have this additional drama in my life and there was a need to let it go and turn it over to God. At that point, I did just that. After going upstairs and noticing that a pillow was out of place on the bed, I picked it up. Replacing the pillow caused a gentle breeze to lift a sheet of paper off the bed, and underneath it was my checkbook. What was on that sheet of paper was so much more significant than just finding the checkbook. Please listen carefully not only with your ears but with your heart.

(Myrtle read the message that was on the sheet. With permission, "The Isolation Chamber" by Bob Gass in *Word for You Today,* has been included.)

Now God is telling us to stop fretting over Elliott's leaving and "Be still and know that He is God." Rejoice in knowing that Elliott is absent from us but present with the Lord.

God bless each and every one of you.

I love you,
Cheryl

The Isolation Chamber

Be still and know that I am God …
—Psalm 46:10 (NIV)

There is a time and place in our walk with God in which He sets us in a place of waiting. It is a place in which all past experiences are of no value. It is a time of such stillness that it can disturb the faithful if we do not understand that He is the One who has brought us to this place for only a season. It is as if God has placed a wall around us. No new opportunities, simply inactivity.

During these times, God is calling us aside to fashion something new in us. It is an isolation chamber designed to call us to deeper roots of faith. It is not a comfortable place, especially for a task-driven businessperson. Our nature cries out, "You must do something." While God is saying, "Be still and know that I am God." You know the signs that you have been brought into this chamber when you can't seem to change anything. Perhaps you are unemployed. Perhaps you are laid up with an illness.

Most religious people live a very planned and orchestrated life where they know almost everything that will happen. But for people in whom God is performing a deeper work, He brings them into a time of quietness that seems almost eerie. They cannot say what God is doing. They just know that He is doing a work that cannot be explained by themselves or others.

Has God brought you to a place of being still? Be still and know that He really is God. When this happens the chamber will open soon after.

Reflecting over the events surrounding Elliott's illness and death has shown me time and time again how God has just wanted me to be still and know that He is God. We all need to realize that fact and truly trust Him.

I have a propensity for misplacing things, resulting in a state of fretfulness and anxiety, as it was with my misplaced checkbook. The more important the item, the more stressed I become when it could not be found. A good example of this occurred while in preparation for the writing of this book.

I used a copy of the original book as a guide in assisting me with my writing. It contained vital irreplaceable information. My heart sank in desperation as I spent days looking for it. I wasn't sure how I would be able to continue without it. I do what I usually do, pray for God to help me find it. But I became more and more anxious with each passing day. The more I looked, the more frustrated and anxious I became.

Had I stopped and remembered 1 Peter 5:7 (NIV), "Cast all your anxiety on God for He cares for you," a lot of anxiety could have been prevented. I put my focus on the lost book instead on the One who knew the location of the book.

After weeks of looking and having feelings of despair, I finally opened a Bible that I had been using, and there was the book. I believe that God has a sense of humor. What a great way to remind me that if you go to the Bible, you will find what you are looking for.

The joy I had in my heart over finding the book was increased with the realization of having another opportunity to trust God in all matters big or small.

After all these years, I am more wiling not to fret and lose my focus as I have in the past.

Thomas and I were blessed to go to Germany to celebrate our precious granddaughter Leona's first birthday. I had packed the same book again to work on the current book while there. I knew I had packed it but could not find it when we arrived. I looked through the entire luggage and it was not there. There was a note placed in my bag stating that my luggage had been randomly selected to be inspected. So I assumed that the book had been taken out during the inspection and had carelessly not been returned to the bag and it was just gone. My response this time was one of calm and trust. I prayed as I usually do and left the concern and anxiety over the lost book with God. I finally got "Be still and know that I am God." When we returned home, I shared with Thomas about the missing book. He reminded me that I had a small carry-on bag in addition to the larger luggage and perhaps it was in there. Sure enough, it was in an outer pocket of the carry-on. My heart rejoiced again, but this time with the greater joy of staying calm and trusting God.

My heart's desire is to encourage you to remember when you are anxious about the issues of life, no matter how big or small they may be, God wants you to be still and know that He is God and has everything under control.

Philippians 4:6–7 (NIV) serves as a reminder.

> Do not be anxious about anything, but in every situation, by prayer and petition, with thanksgiving, present your requests to God.
> And the peace of God, which transcends all understanding, will guard your hearts and your minds in Christ Jesus.

Point to Ponder

Being still and knowing that God is God and He is in total control will give you a divine sense of His presence, which will lead to a more peaceful life.

I want to share a poem written by my brother, Rev. Dr. Lonnell E. Johnson.

BE STILL AND KNOW

Be still, and know that I am God;
I will be exalted among the nations,
I will be exalted in the earth!

—Psalm 46:10 (NIV)

Be still and know that I am God, that I am the eternal One.
Though your cherished dreams have faded and long since gone
The way of all flesh, my divine plans you shall see,

As I weave the tapestry of eternity.
Though you seem forsaken you are never alone,
Even when the burden of dark sin cannot atone,
And the hearts of men have hardened and turned to stone:
Be still and know that I am God.

Though storms may overwhelm and friends may abandon
When diseases surface to assault flesh and bone.
These scenes will reveal the person I thought I could be,
As words of the psalmist comfort and remind me,
When this life is over and all is said and done:
Be still and know that I am God.

Believing

Everything the

Savior says is

Truth

Instilled by His

Love and

Loyalty

Assurance with

No

Doubt

Knowing to

Never

Oppose His

Wisdom

Journey Reflections

Consider the following questions your journey reflection:

Be Still and Know That I Am God

1. What does "Be still and know that I am God" mean to you?

2. Give a specific experience when you needed to be still and seek God's presence.

3. Give reasons why someone would find it difficult to be be still and trust God.

4. Do you feel that it is important to be still and know God? (Why or why not?)

MILE MARKER 11
Acceptance of God's Will

And we know that all things work together for good
to those who love God and are called according to His
purpose.

—Romans 8:28 (NIV)

As my journey has continued, I have become even more keenly aware of
the importance of mile marker 11, "Acceptance of God's Will."

We are reminded in 1 Thessalonians 5:18 (NIV), "Give thanks in all
circumstances, for this is God's will for you in Christ Jesus."

One may question, "How can I give thanks for the heartache,
disappointments, and tragedies of life?"

What God is telling us is to be thankful *in* these situations, no matter
how difficult it may seem. When you have a personal relationship with
God, and you have declared Jesus to be your Lord and Savior, you
believe Romans 8:28 (ESV) without any reservations. "And know that
for those who love God, all things work together for good, for those
who are called according to His purpose." Do you love God? Are you
called according to His purpose? If so, you have a blessed assurance that
all things will work out for your good and God's glory.

Those who do not have that relationship must face trials and tribulations depending on their own abilities. We know for a fact that human power is limited. God's power is limitless. This is one of the most important reasons to establish a personal relationship with God, if you have not already done so.

God wants all of us to be saved. Salvation will help us to deal with this life but more importantly to prepare us to receive eternal life, which should be everyone's ultimate goal.

Accepting of God's will, with the understanding that God loves you and wants only the best for you, will provide what is needed to handle whatever circumstances you must face in this fallen world.

Salvation does not guarantee that that you won't have difficulties, for everyone will as long as they are on this side of heaven. What is guaranteed is the promise that God will be with you. His Word in Hebrews 13:5 (NIV) says, "I will never leave you nor forsake you." God keeps His promises!

Only God knows how many days we are appointed to be here on this earth. Therefore, it is important to value each day and learn to accept whatever His will is for our lives.

Imagine having this enormous picture in front of you. But your eyes are limited to focusing only on one small corner. God has the entire picture in His vision. He knows what is happening in the small realm that you are focused on. Accepting His will can bring the entire picture into clear view at the end of your journey. Only then will you understand why accepting His will is so important.

Won't you accept His will for your life today, and all of your days you are blessed to have? You can trust that God knows exactly what He is doing.

Point to Ponder

God's will is what is best for me!

Always relinquishing

Concerns and having

Confidence that

Every

Problem

To be

Addressed will be

Never forgetting who has total

Control over

Everything

Journey Reflections

Consider the following questions for your journey reflection:

Acceptance of God's Will

1. Is accepting God's will for your life a difficult decision for you? (Explain why or why not.)

2. How can you confuse your will and God's will? (Explain.)

3. How do you know that you are in God's will? (Explain.)

4. Has there been a time when your will and God's will did not agree? What was the outcome? (If not, explain how it would be possible to fight against God's will.)

The Victory Is Always Won with God

> For whatever is born of God overcomes the world. And this is the victory that has overcome the world—our faith.
>
> —1 John 5:4 (NAV)

In Chronicles of Praise: A Life Journey through Death, mile marker 12 symbolized the end of journey for Elliott and me as a couple and the reality of a new beginning for us both.

Now I look at mile marker 12 as a continuation of the life journey God has placed me on since Elliott's death: the rest of the story.

I continue to embrace how very precious life is. I am better equipped to continue on until the end of my earthly journey. These twelve mile markers will continue to serve as a guide to get me home safely. As I continue to travel, God has required of me to serve Him, worship Him, and encourage those He puts on my path to know Him better.

It is my prayer that this book has been an encouragement in some way. Perhaps you were encouraged by some thought that I shared, a scripture, a "Point to Ponder," an acronym, or a question that helped you to reflect on your journey.

I sincerely use these mile markers to help me to navigate through the complexities of this sometimes tumultuous world. My desire is that you will reap a beneficial dividend from the time you invested in reading my story.

God has blessed me so tremendously, and I know He wants me to be a blessing and an encouragement to others.

It is also my prayer that you will diligently seek the Lord, making Him the head of your life, and not wait until you are faced with some of life's most difficult challenges to establish a relationship with Him. For when the storms of life are raging, there is peace knowing that God is already there to give you the victory, no matter how devastating the circumstances may appear.

If you have not given your life to Christ, please take this moment do so now. Heed the words in Romans 10:9 (NIV). "That if you confess with your mouth, Jesus is Lord and believe in your heart that God raised from the dead, you will be saved." Please don't wait, for tomorrow isn't promised to any of us!

John 3:16 (NIV) states,

> For God so loved the world that He gave His only Son, that whoever believes in Him shall not perish, but have eternal life. For God did not send His Son into the world to condemn the world; but to save the world through Him.

First John 5:11–15 (NIV) reassures us of our salvation.

> And this is the testimony: that God hath given us eternal life, and this life is in His Son.
>
> He who has the Son has life; he who does not have the Son of God does not have life. These things I have written to you who believe in the name of the Son of God. That you may know that you have eternal life, and that you may continue to believe in the name of the Son of God.
>
> Now this is the confidence that we have in Him that if we ask anything according to His will, He hears us. And if we know that He hears us, whatever we ask, we know that we have the petitions that we have asked of Him.

God wants us to be saved. He has shown us how to be saved. It is up to us to grasp the opportunity now. Yesterday is gone, tomorrow isn't promised, all we have is today, and that is why we call it the present, which in reality is a gift from God.

I greatly appreciate being able to share the rest of my story with you. It is my prayer that this book has been a help and reassurance of God's love.

I will continue my life's journey in peace with confidence in knowing that one day I will arrive safely home.

What I want more than anything is to meet our Savior face-to-face and hear Jesus say, "Well done, my good and faithful servant."

I pray that your life journey will also be full of God's love, grace, peace, joy, and favor.

Please be an encouragement to others.

Always remember and never forget that with God, you have the victory!

Point to Ponder

Don't wait until the battle is over. Shout right now. Know that God is working it out for your good and His glory.

#thefightisfixedandyouhavethevictory
#Godgivesusthevictory
#victoryismine

Validation

In having the

Confidence of knowing

That

Our Savior

Really loves you and

You are the winner!

Journey Reflections

Consider the following questions for your journey reflection:

The Victory Is Always Won with God

1. Do you believe that the victory is always won with God? (Explain.)

2. Can you be victorious without God's help? (Explain.)

3. What victories have you received which you know that only God could have been responsible for them? (Explain.)

4. What can you do to prepare for the final victory, eternal life? (Be specific.)

Chronicles of Praise: Facebook Reflections

As a response to all of the love and support Elliott and I received during our final year together, I started sending out email messages that I called "Praise Reports." Unintentionally, our yearlong journey was chronicled. As an afterthought, I would include the "Praise Reports" at the end of the *Chronicles of Praise: A Life Journey through Death.* The book was published in 2004. Ironically that was the year Facebook started.

I didn't join Facebook until 2009. It served as a replacement for the many emails I used to send. Facebook has been an integral part of my life since joining. I have used it as my platform to encourage, support, inspire, offer prayer, seek prayer, and spread love. All that I have given out, I have so graciously received in return.

When I reviewed many of my posts that I have made over the years, I see how the twelve mile markers have been a positive influence over my thinking. When I decided that I wanted to share some of my favorite posts at the end of this book, it was an easy task to incorporate them into the mile markers.

May these selected reflections serve as an ever-present help and reassurance of the power of words to encourage. May you find encouragement and inspiration in the following "Facebook Reflections":

MILE 1: HOPE

October 23, 2015

Not sure whom this is for but God and you know! Thank You, Lord, for allowing the eyes and hearts that need this special encouragement from You which you have placed on my heart so strongly today to read this ...

"Keep your hope alive! For as long as you have hope you have life and as long as you have life you have hope! Don't give in now! Things are about to change in your favor!"

My work here is done. Wait ... Just got another confirmation that this message is needed. The song "It's Not Over" is playing.

MILE MARKER 2: FAITH

October 4, 2010

> Now faith is the substance of things hoped for and the evidence of things not seen … But without faith it is impossible to please God. (Hebrews 11:1, 6 KJV)

Give yourself a "faith lift" this week, and God will be pleased.

October 25, 2017

So grateful that God is so faithful! He is the same yesterday, today, and tomorrow! He always has the final say! Somebody besides me needs this timely reminder. Be encouraged!

Mile Marker 3: Courage

November 5, 2010

Only God can turn a mess into a message. So if you are in a mess or dealing with mess, just know that God has a message of hope, deliverance, and victory!

November 18, 2013

Words of encouragement: Life can change in the blink of an eye. But rest assured that God never blinks! No matter what, know without a shadow of a doubt that God cares about you and what you are going through. So hold tightly to God's unchanging hand, and walk through the pain, hurt, disappointment, and confusion of why, with our ever-faithful, peace-giving, nonblinking God. He will carry you through!

January 14, 2018

God is going to work it out! Don't be afraid!

Mile Marker 4: Family and Friends

July 16, 2015

I was just looking at my list of Facebook friends and again I am reminded how very blessed I am! Thanks for being my friend!

November 12, 2015

One of the best parts of celebrating my birthday is receiving all of the birthday love on Facebook! I appreciate every post, prayer, and thought! When I say that, "I am so blessed, highly favored, and grateful!" you are such a great reason that I say it, and really mean it. Thank you for being such an important part of my life. As I frequently say when wishing others a happy birthday, "May this be your best year ever!" I receive those words for myself. Having you there is a reassurance that this will be the best year ever!

Mile Marker 5: Communicate Your Thoughts

September 25, 2015

I am led by the Spirit to share something said to me by a friend who had a powerful impact on my life. Yes, words have power! I am going to share it with all who will receive it. Throughout the day, say these words and mean it: "Speak, Lord. I am listening! Thank You!" Say it especially in the time of confusion and doubt about what to do. Be aware that God speaks in so many different ways. So you must pay attention while you are listening for Him. Showing gratitude is essential!

May this make a difference in your day and your life as it has in mine. Thank you, Andrea, for what I know God gave to you to share with me. Thank you, Lord, for speaking. I am listening!

August 27, 2019

Never trust your tongue, when your heart is bitter or broken. Hush until you are healed.

September 23, 2019

Lord, please put Your arm around my shoulder and Your hand over my mouth!

September 26, 2019

Today will never come again …
Be a blessing.
Be a friend.
Take time to care.
Take time to love.
Let your words heal and not hurt.

October 21, 2019

Not My Job	**My Job**
Fix or save people.	Love people.
Be liked.	Be kind.
Do it all.	Pray for all.
Please everyone.	Please try to lead everyone to Christ.
Hold it all together.	Depend on God to keep it together until I get it together.

Mile Marker 6: Read and Believe God's Word

November 15, 2010

Thought for the Week

> Trust in the Lord with all thine heart; and lean not unto thine own understanding. In all thy ways acknowledge Him and He shall direct thy paths. (Proverbs 3:5–6 KJV)

Let the Lord lead!

February 12, 2018

911 Emergency Scriptures
(Can be used in non-emergencies)

- Reassurance: Psalm 91:1
- Need courage: Deuteronomy 31:6
- Need financial help: Philippians 4:19
- Upset: John 14:1
- Lonely: Psalm 23
- Worried: Matthew 6:25–34
- Sinned: Psalm 51
- Grieving: 1 Thessalonians 4:13–18
- Traveling: Psalm 121
- When God seems far: Psalm 9:10

- Concern for the future: Jeremiah 29:11
- Seeking peace: Numbers 6:24–26
- Need direction: Proverbs 3:5–6
- Depression: Psalm 27
- Protection: 2 Thessalonians 3:3–5
- Anxious: Romans 8:31–35
- Bitter and critical: 1 Corinthians 13
- Hope: Romans 15:13
- Danger: Psalm 91
- Fear: Isaiah 41:10

Mile Marker 7: Prayer

September 5, 2011

Lord, help us to stand in the gap for and not in the way of each other. Pray for each other for we all are fighting a battle of one kind or another. Prayer can and does change things!

July 6, 2015

Prayer is the key to heaven, but faith unlocks the door!

September 15, 2019

Worry is a conversation you have with yourself about things you cannot change.
Prayer is a conversation you have with God about things He can change.

Mile Marker 8: The Fruit of the Spirit

June 16, 2015

Happy birthday to my wonderful mother, who would be celebrating her ninety-fifth earthly birthday but now is celebrating her thirteenth birthday in heaven. I had to do the math for it is hard to believe those numbers! It is amazing how quickly time has passed. Yet the precious memories have not faded one bit. I am so grateful for all her wonderful traits that she has instilled in me. I am more loving, kind, generous, forgiving, and so full of faith because of watching how she lived. Thank You, Lord, for choosing me to be Jessie Marie Johnson's grateful daughter. I encourage myself as I encourage so many others whose mothers have gone home to be with the Lord to focus on the good memories instead of her not being here. I am one blessed woman!

Mile Marker 9: Trust God

June 4, 2011

Go into the weekend knowing that the Lord has your back! No matter what it looks like, God has a totally different perspective. Don't worry. He has you!

October 8, 2014

Not sure who this is for besides me. God just dropped this in my Spirit so strong that I had to stop putting up my groceries so I could share it immediately!

God said, "I have not forgotten you! Don't be discouraged! Trust Me! It is going to happen in my time. I love you! Keep praying. I am listening!"

I think my work here is done now. Keep the faith, and believe!

God's got this!

September 22, 2019

Whatever you need, God will supply, so stop fretting! God is aware, and He is in control.

Mile Marker 10: Be Still and Know That I Am God

June 2, 2015

Let me share the confirmation from God that I just got from a friend who sent this just because the Spirit prompted her. I know God wants me to share this with someone else who is going through some sort of storm. If you are not, then you should be praising the Lord and praying for us who are ...

> God is stirring the waters! We serve a God who delights in doing amazing things in the lives of His people. Not only does He want to amaze you, but He also wants the watching world to see His miracle-working power manifested in your life!
>
> Don't give up praying and believing for the breakthrough you need, whether in your health, your finances, your emotions, or your family. He is offering to empower you to do the impossible. This can be your breakthrough moment. God is already stirring the healing waters for you today ... Opening awesome doors for you to receive the fullness of His salvation, deliverance, abundance, and healing and eternal life. So go ahead and jump into the miracle water so you can receive the supernatural breakthrough you need. Get ready for your miracle! Live to love! Live in peace! Have faith in God!

I am so encouraged, and I hope it does the same for you.

Mile Marker 11: Acceptance of God's Will

December 31, 2013

Food for thought: I ran across a note from God that He wants me to share with you.

> Good afternoon,
>
> You were not born with the spirit of fear, and I will never leave or forsake you. I will be handling your problems today and throughout the New Year. It may not feel like it or look like it, but I am working it for your breakthrough. The only thing I will need from you is to trust in Me. So relax, and have a great day and great year!
>
> Your Heavenly Father,
> God

June 2, 2015

Thank You, God, for the peace in the middle of this storm!

I am so confident that God has worked all of this out for my good and His glory! I don't know how, don't know when, but what I do know is that I have the victory! Pray for me and with me while we wait to see how God is going to fix it! And He will! Pardon me while I praise Him right in the middle of this!

Mile Marker 12: The Victory Is Always Won with God

October 29, 2013

Not sure who this is for besides me, but I felt the need to share this: "When things don't work out the way you wanted them to, just know that God has a better plan! Trust Him and His plan! I needed that!"

June 8, 2015

I am not going to wait until the battle is over to shout! I am going to shout right now! God is working on my behalf as I write. I can say with the utmost confidence that I have the victory. Come on and praise Him with me! Can you say hallelujah? Thank You, Jesus!

June 29, 2015

The song "I Just Want to Praise You" by Maurette Brown Clark says it all! I just want to praise the Lord for the victory!

When it looked like I wasn't going to win this battle, I held on and believed, and God came through again! Let me encourage those who are going through to hold on, for your victory is coming too! We are overcomers by the blood of the Lamb and the word of our testimony. I am here to testify that there is nothing too hard for God! No matter what it looks like, keep your eyes on God and let Him work it out! I have been shouting and praising all day!

August 5, 2018

God said, "Everything is going to be all right!"

Being confident of this very thing, that He Who has begun a good work in you will complete it until the day of Jesus Christ. (Philippians 1:6 NIV)

Printed in the United States
By Bookmasters